MINI MYTHS
TALES FROM ANCIENT GREECE

MYTHICAL
MONSTERS

Beatrice Cope

PURPLE TOAD
PUBLISHING

P.O. Box 631
Kennett Square, Pennsylvania 19348
www.purpletoadpublishing.com

Printing
1   2   3   4   5   6   7   8   9

Fabulous Fables
Heroic Heroes
The Labors of Hercules
Mythical Monsters
Tantalizing Tales

Publisher's Cataloging-in-Publication Data
Cope, Beatrice
  Mythical monsters / Beatrice Cope
     p. cm. – (A Tommy tiger book. Mini myths tales for Ancient Greece)
Includes bibliographic references and index.
ISBN: 978-1-62469-003-7 (library bound)
1. Mythology, Greek – Juvenile literature.   I. Title.
  BL783.C674 2013
  398.2093'8—dc23
                                                          2013930982

eBook ISBN: 978-1-62469-014-3

ABOUT THE AUTHOR: Beatrice Cope has taught English in universities and private schools across the country. Her play, *The Magic Horse,* was performed at the University of Chicago. This is her first book.

PUBLISHER'S NOTE: The mythology in this book has been researched in depth, and to the best of our knowledge is correct. Although every measure is taken to give an accurate account, Purple Toad Publishing makes no warranty of the accuracy of the information and is not liable for damages caused by inaccuracies.

Printed by Lake Book Manufacturing, Chicago, IL

CONTENTS

THE
CYCLOPES

On a mountaintop which touched the sky
Lived the Cyclopes, giants with one eye.
Only one eye, ugly and horrid,
Which sat in the middle of
Each ugly forehead.

They lived all alone, without father or mother,
The Cyclopes liked no one,
Not even each other!

These terrible giants were an awful danger,
They wouldn't think twice about harming a stranger.
What would they do to him?
How would they treat him?
They'd CRRRRRRRUNCH up his bones,
And then slow-ly eat him!

Do we worry about Cyclopes? Not today.
A long time ago, they all went away.

THE
GRAY SISTERS

Imagine three sisters, lovely of face,
Pretty to look at, with swanlike grace.
But strange to know, and stranger to say,
From the time they were born,
Their hair was gray.

And then beyond this scary sight,
They had one tooth with which to bite.
One tooth, that is, amongst the three—
So they passed it around
Most carefully.

They also shared but just one eye,
They would moan and shriek and loudly cry,
"My turn! My turn! My turn to see!
I want the eye,
Give it to me!"

And being blind, they'd flail and fight,
Wanting a turn at glorious sight.
And while they wrestled,
Each trying to grab it,
One sister would win and
NAB it!

And the others, jealous, would scream
for the eye.
If they weren't careful and didn't mind,
They would drop the eye and
ALL would be blind.

Weird sisters, fighting, hitting, not caring,
They'd do much better to be sharing.

THE
CHIMAERA

Would you like to be chased by a bad-tempered goat?
Or by a lion with a thick shaggy coat?
Would you run from a dragon,
Breathing hot fire—
One who whips around fast and never gets tired?

The monster Chimaera has three hungry heads:
In the front, a lion; on her back, a mean goat;
And scorching hot flames pour from each nasty throat.
Her serpent tail swishes as she gallops fast
So hide behind a rock
And watch her
fly past.

CERBERUS

At the gates of the land of the mythical dead
Sits a fearsome watchdog with three horrible heads.
One head looks left,
One to the right,
With one in the middle:
He's a terrible sight!

"GGGRRR" growls head one,
"Snarl" snaps head two
The third one roars with the sound of a zoo.
His eyes flash with sparks,
But watch for his tail,
Which is a great serpent covered with scale.
He is very frightening to be around.
Good thing Cerberus lives
Far underground.

SCYLLA AND CHARYBDIS

High on a cliff overlooking the ocean,
Sits a restless monster, always in motion.
With six grisly heads, twelve hands, and
    twelve feet,
She snatches poor sailors,
To chew
To gnaw
To eat!

If Scylla doesn't pluck them as they are sailing by,
The whirlpool Charybdis will give it a try.
She sucks their ships 'round, 'round, and way down
    under,
Then spews them back up with the sound of thunder.

Scylla and Charybdis are wild, and fierce, and mean,
One must be very careful not to get between.

Note: Don't get between a rock and a hard place.

CENTAURS

Everyone loves ponies, and, of course,
There's nothing more wonderful
Than a horse.
But mythical horses, half man, half beast,
Caused big trouble, to say the least.

They had great strength and terrible might,
And loved to drink and start a fight.
If there were a party or any festival,
They would appear, savage and bestial.
Because they could not be good and quiet,
Wherever they went
They caused a riot.

In a twisting labyrinth built in a cave,
The Minotaur lurked and roared and raved.
He was a man in front, in back a bull,
He was strong and fierce
And built to kill!

Every nine years, he was given to eat
Seven boys and seven girls—for him a treat.
Till a hero named Theseus cried, "This must stop!
Send *me* to the monster, I'll give him a
BOP!"

So Theseus stalked through the cave,
Looking left and right,
Til he came to the Minotaur, a terrible sight!
But Theseus was lucky, the monster was napping—
So he hit him hard, no gentle tapping!

And the Minotaur slept on,
In fact he was dead;
All from a very hard BOP on the head.
Now he no longer roars
And he no longer eats
Boys and girls—
not even as treats!

PAN

If you like noise and singing and dancing,
Join Pan in the woods and start your prancing.
He's a goat man, with horns parting his curls,
And wherever he goes follow woodland girls.

He plays a flute and the girls dance after,
With shouting and singing and bubbly laughter.

Pan is wild; he is never quiet,
Wherever he goes, he starts a riot.

It is called "pandemonium."

THE
SPHINX

There once was a beast with the face of a girl.
Her hair hung down in long silky curls.
She had a lion's body and an eagle's wings.
She didn't look monstrous
But
She did monstrous things!

She sat by a road that led to a city
And questioned each traveler without any pity.
She asked them a riddle, and if they could not think,
She picked them up
And ATE them, all in a wink!

She ate men by the dozen, leaving bones galore.,
But when one had the answer,
She didn't eat any more!

What happened to the sphinx is not quite clear from
  history,

We know she killed herself, but how remains a
   mystery.
The Riddle: What walks on four legs in the
   morning, two in the middle of the
   day, and three in the evening?
The Answer: Man. He crawls when a baby, the
   moning of his life, walks on two legs when
   grown,
   and uses a cane when he is old.

THE
SATYRS

Satyrs were certainly strange-looking creatures,
With beards and horns and craggy features.
They lived in the woods,
In fields and near streams,
They   played flutes and pipes and tambourines.
Their feet were hooves with which they pranced,
Though if you asked, they'd say they danced.
Satyrs were noisy and a little evil,
Most people would say they were primeval.

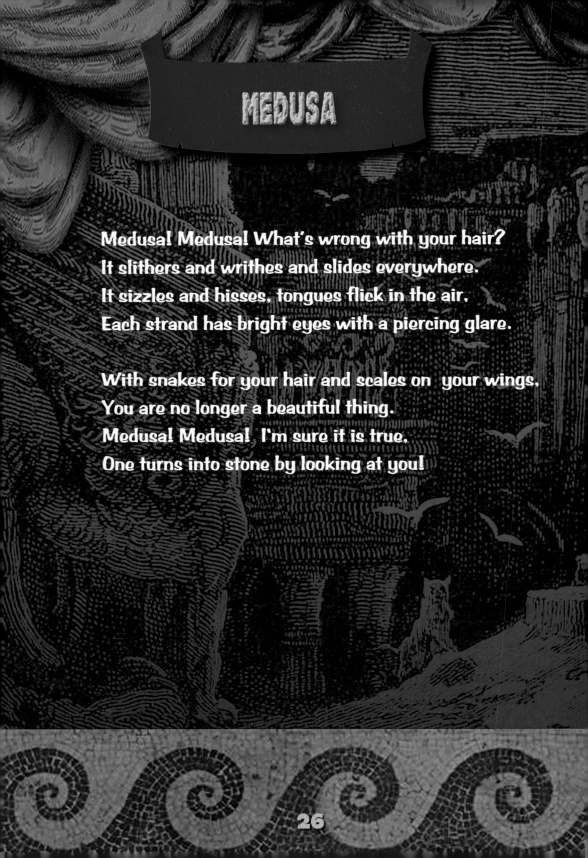

MEDUSA

Medusa! Medusa! What's wrong with your hair?
It slithers and writhes and slides everywhere.
It sizzles and hisses, tongues flick in the air,
Each strand has bright eyes with a piercing glare.

With snakes for your hair and scales on your wings,
You are no longer a beautiful thing.
Medusa! Medusa! I'm sure it is true,
One turns into stone by looking at you!

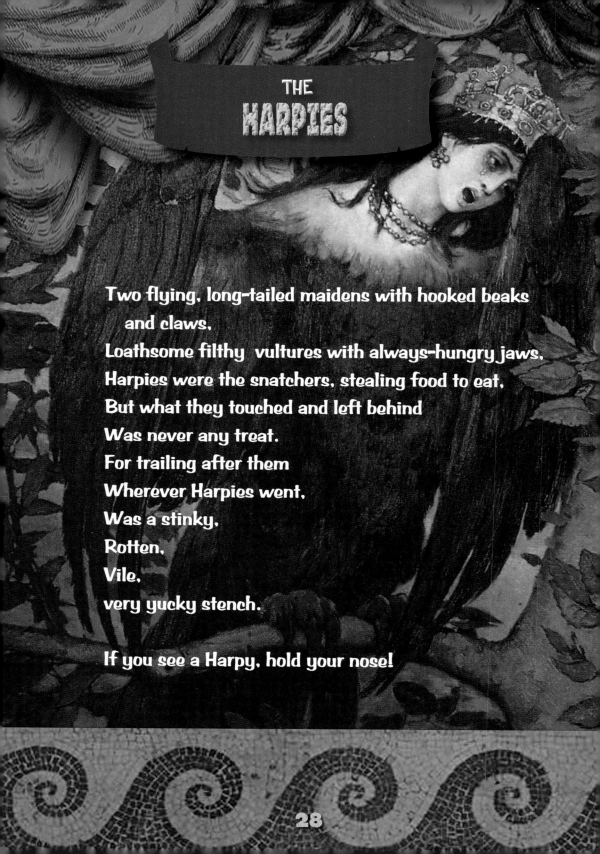

THE
HARPIES

Two flying, long-tailed maidens with hooked beaks
   and claws,
Loathsome filthy vultures with always-hungry jaws,
Harpies were the snatchers, stealing food to eat,
But what they touched and left behind
Was never any treat.
For trailing after them
Wherever Harpies went,
Was a stinky,
Rotten,
Vile,
very yucky stench.

If you see a Harpy, hold your nose!

PROTEUS

When you've been a little naughty,
   And your mom is scolding you,
You can pretend you're Proteus,
   And turn into a zoo.

When Mother grabs you by the hand,
   Change into a tree.
Think thoughts of "cool and leafy"
   And how puzzled she will be.

When she puts you in the tub,
   Turn into a fish,
And when she is not looking,
   Give your tail a swish.

When you try to run away
   And she comes running after,
Turn into a prowling panther,
   And growl amid the laughter.

If she should scold you at the store,
    Because you're always lagging,
Dare to have a little fun
    And turn into a dragon.

And when the day is over,
    And night begins to fall,
Be your own loveable person
    The best shape of them all.

Books

Alexander, Heather. *A Child's Introduction to Greek Mythology*. New York: Black Dog & Leventhal, 2011.

d'Aulaire, Ingri, and Edgar Perrin D'Aulaire. *D'Aulaire's Book of Greek Myths*. New York: Delacorte Books for Young Readers, 1992.

Napoli, Donna Jo. *National Geographic Treasury of Greek Mythology*. Des Moines, IA: National Geographic Children's Books, 2011.

On the Internet

Greek Mythology
http://www.mythweb.com/

Greek Mythology for Kids
http://greece.mrdonn.org/myths.html

Works Consulted

Bulfinch, Thomas. *Bulfinch's Mythology: The Age of Fable*. Garden City, NY: Doubleday and Sons, 1968.

Day, Malcolm. *100 Characters from Classical Mythology*. Hauppauge, NY: Barron's Educational Series, 2007.

Evslin, Bernard. *Heroes, Gods and Monsters of the Greek Myths*. New York: Random House Children's Books, 2005.

Hamilton, Edith. *Mythology*. Boston: Little, Brown and Company, 1942, 1969.

Morford, Mark P.O., Robert J. Lenardon, and Michael Sham. *Classical Mythology*. Ninth Edition. New York: Oxford University Press, 2010.